WHITE

BY **JAMES IJAMES**

★

★

DRAMATISTS
PLAY SERVICE
INC.

WHITE was developed at the PlayPenn New Play Conference (Paul Meshejian, Artistic Director).

The development of this play was supported by the Philadelphia Theatre Company (Paige Price, Producing Artistic Director; Melissa Zimmerman, Interim Managing Director) through the Terrence McNally Award for New Plays.

WHITE received its world premiere at Theatre Horizon (Erin Reilly, Artistic Director; Molly Braverman, Managing Director; Jennifer Pratt Johnson, Executive Director) in Norristown, Pennsylvania, opening on May 3, 2017. It was directed by Malika Oyetimein, the scenic design was by Colin McIlvaine, the lighting design was by Mike Inwood, the costume design was by LeVonne Lindsay, the sound design was by Larry Fowler, the prop design was by Chris Haig, and the stage manager was Chelsea Sanz. The cast was as follows:

GUS .... Jamison Foreman
VANESSA .... Jaylene Clark Owens
JANE .... Jessica Bedford
TANNER .... Justin Jain

ACKNOWLEDGMENTS

PlayPenn
Gulfshore Playhouse
Wilma Theatre

SPECIAL THANKS

Lucie Tiberghien
Joniece Abbott Pratt
Ben Pelteson
Elaina Di Monaco

CHARACTERS

GUS—An Artist. White male. 30s.

VANESSA—The Actress. A Black woman. 20s–30s.
　　Also ST. DIANA OF DETROIT—A vision.
　　　　Later BALKONAÉ TOWNSEND—An artist.

JANE—The Curator. White female. 30s.

TANNER—The Boyfriend. Asian male. Late 20s – early 30s.

NOTES

Unless otherwise indicated, dialogue should be continuous without pauses.

/ indicates overlapping text.

… indicates the attempt and the failure to complete a thought. Not so much a trailing off.

— indicates a cut off or interruption of a thought.

Beat—Exactly as long as it takes you to say *beat* in your head.

Silence—Speaking without words.

On style: This play should feel like a sitcom until it's not. Fast while remaining grounded. Broad while remaining specific.

On space: This play works best when the production does not attempt to place each location. Allow the actors to establish where, when, and what we are looking at. A big open space that can be everywhere and everything is ideal.

"…don't be afraid of your shadows having white in them…"

—James Abbott McNeill Whistler

"Genius is personal, decided by fate, but it expresses itself by means of system. There is no work of art without system."

—Le Corbusier

"You think you slick, but you ain't slick enough to slide."

—African American Proverb

Damn Skippy!

WHITE

1.

Jane stands holding a glass of champagne in a slash of stage light. She taps the side of the glass to get the room's attention.

JANE. Hello. Hi. I'm Jane Forsyth, senior curator here at the Parnell Museum, and I want to thank you all for coming tonight to the opening of this extraordinary exhibition of spectacular work by a group of very exciting new American artists. The Parnell Museum for Contemporary American Art has been the foremost museum of its kind in the country. Founded at the end of the Second World War the museum has showcased the works of the best and brightest. When I came to the Parnell, the perspective was decidedly homogenous. I have spent this year searching for new perspectives. New voices. New work! Challenging and interesting art that would keep the Parnell at the very front of the art world nationally and internationally. I would like to begin with some history. Lights.

> *She clicks a slide.*
>
> *Slide: A painting of men standing in line. All dressed working class. Communist feeling.*

This is Marshall Kaiterman. 1996. It's called *The Old Line.*

> *Slide: An actual cup of coffee. A half-eaten piece of toast.*

This is Felix Mueller. 1999. It's called *mon petit déjeuner.*

> *Slide: A photo of a woman with no pants on trying to hail a cab.*

Jensen. 2009. Called *Easy Breezy Beautiful.*

> *Slide: A chair with no seat.*

Barvel. 2013. Called *Chair Étude No. 9.*

Slide: A painting of a child with enormous green eyes.

Schiele. 2012. Not to be confused with Egon Schiele. This one is called *Peek a Boo Boo.*

All of these artists have two things in common. They all have works that are permanent acquisitions of the Parnell and they are all white men. This show. This New America Exhibition is the first chapter in changing the current face of this institution. New America reflects the full range of America.

2.

Lights expand out to include Gus entering. He has a glass of champagne in one hand and a large painting under his other arm. We are instantly in his studio. This exchange should feel old and comfortable. They may have had a few drinks by now.

GUS. Hegemony.

JANE. Oh! That's a good one!

GUS. Heteronormative.

JANE. Yes! Oh I've got one! Unpack!

GUS. Wait a minute!

JANE. I know that's one of your go-to things to say…but…UGH!!!!

GUS. ExCUSE me! It's a good word.

JANE. If I hear that word one more time! Unpack! Aren't you people all moved in now! Must we continuously UNPACK everything?

GUS. Yes! The word bears repeating! UNPACK!

JANE. It's a buzz word! Like…

GUS. "Problematize"?

JANE. and…"curate"!

GUS. You're a curator!

JANE. So is everyone else! The barista this morning…? Curator. He told me that they were "curating" their pastries so I couldn't have the apple fritter I have been getting for years! Curating pastries. Fucking idiocy in a green apron. I hate it.

GUS. You haven't changed one bit. Same Jane Forsyth! Storming the castle! Railing against misogyny and irony and…what else was it?

JANE. Paisley, I think!

GUS. And now you're burning barns at the FUCKING PARNELL!

JANE. Yes!

GUS. Yeeeeees! That show of yours is getting a lot of buzz!

JANE. Mmhmm…

    Silence.

So…Where's Tanner?

GUS. Staying late at school. He's directing the middle-school production of *Julius Caesar*.

JANE. That sounds supremely terrible. Aaaaaaaaw. I was hoping to see him! You know you lucked up right?

GUS. Fully aware.

JANE. Good! Don't screw it up!

GUS. So…

JANE. Yeah?

GUS. Your first big show!

JANE. Yeah. Oh! There is this kid out of CalArts that is just dynamite. He can't be more than like 23.

GUS. Wow…that's…young.

JANE. I know. He's Colombian and Chinese!

GUS. Really?

JANE. Right! How does that happen? Anyway he's great!

GUS. Clearly.

JANE. What's new with you?

GUS. Been painting a lot.

JANE. I can see. A lot of new stuff around here.

GUS. Yeah. I got that Meredith Fellowship.

JANE. That's right. Congrats! I'm sorry I meant to say that when I arrived.

GUS. No worries.

JANE. So you're not teaching right now?

GUS. Yeah. I've taken the year off.

JANE. Good for you! Good! You should be painting full time. I love your stuff, Gus! Oh my god! Do you remember that performance art thingy we did in grad school in the library! We were crazy!

GUS. Yeah. We were. Wheeeewww.

JANE. Wacky!

GUS. Yeah.

> *They go silent. They sip their champagne.*

JANE. Glad you're being prolific!

GUS. Thanks. Hey. Check this one out.

> *Gus grabs the painting he brought in and props it up for Jane to look at. Jane examines the painting. The painting is very white. Metallic raised white lines moving from the four corners of the canvas towards the center. They are laid out on a matte-finish white canvas. The work is minimalist and striking.*

JANE. Oh Gus.

GUS. It's good, right?

JANE. Yeah! Although this feels…like…it could use more color?

GUS. Okay.

JANE. You use white a lot and that's great…I just wish there were more…blue. Or something.

GUS. Blue?

JANE. Yes. The color blue.

GUS. Why blue?

JANE. Hey…We're honest with each other. We tell each other the truth right?

GUS. Yes!

JANE. More blue.

GUS. Oh okay. Well…I'm trying to explore the intersection between my white body, hence the abundance of white, and my gay body, hence...

He points out something phallic perhaps in the paint?

These two parts of me are ever in conversation with each other but are never totally listening to each other. The ability to have access and also restriction all in the same being. I'm trying to find this in the line and the starkness of the canvas. It's all building to converge at the center. Here.

JANE. I can see that.

GUS. The Fellowship has given me so much time! I can really push the boundaries of the work.

JANE. Mmhmm.

GUS. I was thinking this could be good for the New America Exhibition.

JANE. Oh...ha...yeah...no.

GUS. Jane you want this piece in the show!

JANE. Gus, I love it. It's really minimalist. And you know how much I love minimalist.

GUS. Yes.

JANE. With that said, I...may I be frank?

GUS. Of course.

JANE. This work is terrific. All of your work is terrific.

GUS. Thank you.

JANE. But it's not actually about that.

GUS. It's not.

JANE. I gave myself a charge when I took this job. I would fundamentally change the face of this museum to truly reflect America.

GUS. Great!

JANE. I'm committed to that Gus!

GUS. Right on Sister!

JANE. So...I can't put you in my first exhibition at the Parnell. You're the exact opposite of what I'm looking for.

GUS. I am?

JANE. Yeah. No white dudes.

GUS. …

…

You think of me as a dude.

JANE. The museum has dozens of artists like you already. I want some new perspectives. New voices. Different voices.

GUS. I'm different.

JANE. Not really.

GUS. Thanks friend.

JANE. See…I didn't want to talk shop with you for this very reason.

GUS. This is what I need Jane! Showing at the Parnell is next level for me.

JANE. You and everyone else.

GUS. So…who's in the show?

JANE. The official selections are not finished yet but—

GUS. —Who.

JANE. Well…let me see…D'Wayne Freeman.

GUS. You're presenting D'wayne Freeman. That guy's not new. He's been around for…Jesus forever.

JANE. He's examining black matriarchy in his work with textiles, digital media, AND metal. It's all very interesting and powerful work. And…well…he's African American.

GUS. Oh…I see… Is that the only criteria?

JANE. Gus—

GUS. —I'M GAY.

JANE. This is uncomfortable.

GUS. Doesn't that count for anything?

JANE. Of course it does. You're my favorite gay!

GUS. You think this queer artist thing is a cake walk?!

JANE. This isn't about who's more marginalized.

GUS. But if I were black, that would increase my chances?

JANE. No. Not necessarily.

GUS. Really?

JANE. No. But I'm not gonna lie, if you were black and female and making the work you are making, it would be perfect.

GUS. Did you really just say that?!

JANE. It's not personal. Geez.

GUS. Right.
(Closer. Resigned.) Right.
(Brighter. Lying.) Alright.

JANE. Hey…Look…I'm a big fan, Gus. You know that. Truly. But… there's just a bit too much chicken sausage over at the museum.

GUS. Chicken sausage?

JANE. White meat.

GUS. I see.

JANE. Next year?

GUS. Yes.

> *Jane leaves.*

3.

> *Instantly we are in the apartment of Gus and boyfriend, Tanner. Tanner sits in a chair and puts his feet up. He is barefooted and grades papers. Gus walks over to him. Tanner looks up from his grading.*

TANNER. Hey you!

GUS. How was your day?

TANNER. The usual. Of course the monsters didn't have their papers.

GUS. Poor poor Professor Put-upon.

TANNER. Come kiss me I don't feel like getting up.

> *Gus does so.*

GUS. What are you working on?

TANNER. Papers for American Lit.

Tanner reads a passage from one of the papers.

Oh Jesus. Listen to this.

(Reads.) "When I had first read *Beloved*, I didn't really like it. But with Mr. Tanner—"

(To Gus.) Like I'm not reading this. I hate kiss ups.

(Reads.) "—with Mr. Tanner explaining all of the intimate details—"

(Writes.) —What details? Please cite examples—

(Reads.) "—I got a fuller understanding of the book and the people in it and what they were there for. I thought to myself, 'Who you to question? Just enjoy the ride.'"

GUS. What's wrong with that?

TANNER. "What they were there for"?!?! And Verbs! What is so wrong with verbs. I like verbs! They make reading so enjoyable.

GUS. You're a snob, you know?

TANNER. *(Sort of snort-laughs at this idea.)* What?

GUS. You're very patrician, Tanner.

> *Tanner full-on laughs.*

You are!

TANNER. This from a man who measures his coffee beans...

GUS. Well you have to get the right density of flavor...

TANNER. And the artisanal mustard of the month membership... what about that?

GUS. I like mustard!

TANNER. Oh and lest we forget about those chevron stripes in the bathroom.

GUS. That's not patrician, that's good taste.

TANNER. Right.

GUS. Okay so we're both particular.

TANNER. English teachers have to be particular. What's your excuse?

GUS. Just love when you pick on me.

TANNER. Me too. How was your day?

GUS. It was okay.

TANNER. *(Back to grading.)* Just okay?

GUS. Yeah.

TANNER. Uh oh.

GUS. What?

TANNER. Not inspired?

GUS. Can't seem to…Paint anything good. Really…

TANNER. The painting you were working on last month. The one with the lines, I LOVED that one. Did you show Jane that one?

GUS. Sure did. Sheeeee doesn't think it fits into her "aesthetic" for her exhibition.

TANNER. Oh No! Babe! I'm sorry. Did she say why?

GUS. Oh yes!

TANNER. Why?

GUS. She's not going to include me because I'm a white dude.

TANNER. She thinks of you as a dude?

GUS. Focus!

TANNER. She just said that? That it was because you're white.

GUS. And male! Don't forget about male.

TANNER. Right.

GUS. Yes.

TANNER. Oh.

GUS. Yeah.

TANNER. I see.

GUS. It's totally fucked up right?

TANNER. I mean… She does this. Remember the all-blind sculptor show? Jane and her crusades.

GUS. That's your response? "Crazy Jane and her fetishes." Whose side are you on?

> Tanner stops and looks at Gus, he sees that Gus is actually troubled. He grows serious.

TANNER. Yours. You know that.

GUS. Isn't that illegal

TANNER. I—

GUS. —I mean if she is going to pick artists based on the immutable characteristics of their birth like their race or gender, what about sexual orientation?

TANNER. I think perhaps she is doing something different.

GUS. Like what?!

…

…

I need you to see where I'm coming from here.

TANNER. I do, Gus. But… You've been really successful. You've been in some really amazing shows. You're doing well. Maybe this is about giving chances to people who don't have the advantages you have.

GUS. I've worked really hard.

TANNER. I know. I'm not saying you haven't.

GUS. I'm good.

TANNER. You are. But there are a lot of good artists.

GUS. I'm really fucking good! I'm great!

TANNER. Gus. No one is denying that.

GUS. Isn't she?

TANNER. I don't think she is. Jane has included your work before.

GUS. I know. But, it's the Parnell. Tanner!

TANNER. Why is this bothering you so much?

GUS. Ugh. Never mind.

TANNER. You know she likes your work.

GUS. Sorry. It's like I'm possessed by this!

TANNER. You're not possessed you're hungry.

GUS. What?

TANNER. You're an asshole when you're hungry. Go eat something.

GUS. But I—

TANNER. —Go.

GUS. Okay.

> *Tanner fades away. Gus is alone when the strings of sublime Motown begin to play. Then, at a celestial distance, in a glorious pool of shimmering blue light, a figure emerges.*

She has massive hair crowned with a luminous halo. Her gown is iridescent blue. It catches and reflects the light. She beckons for Gus. He turns and sees her. She is just out of his reach. This is Saint Diana. Gus is blown away by her. It should feel sublime, frightening, and holy all at once. Gus approaches her.

DIANA. Gus.

GUS. Yes.

DIANA. Gus!

GUS. Yes!

DIANA. Gus McKnight!!

GUS. Yes! Yes!

DIANA. I'm here for you. If you ever need me. Call me.

GUS. Who are you? Are you my fairy godmother?

DIANA. No.

GUS. Hallucination?

DIANA. I...am Saint Diana.

GUS. Ms. Ross?

DIANA. The Boss.

GUS. Cheese and rice.

DIANA. I am the perfect personification of the beautiful black woman you have nurtured inside you! Hear my voice Gus, and hear me good. See me! I am ever here! Always by your side.

GUS. Yes.

DIANA. I've been watching you. I've been feeling your distress. So I thought I would reach out and touch you. I have come to give you guidance and comfort.

GUS. What should I do?

DIANA. You must harness the magic within yourself and create something fierce.

GUS. I don't understand.

DIANA. You have been nurturing something inside that is crying to get out. Unleash your full potential my son.

GUS. Yes, Diana.

DIANA. Gus, Gus, Gus.

GUS. Yes, Yes, Yes.

DIANA. Believe...In yourself.

GUS. Yeah Yeah Yeah.

DIANA. Get *yours* my son.

GUS. What's that mean?

DIANA. Make...that paper, player.

GUS. Is that like a riddle?

DIANA. "Get dat money!" as they say.

GUS. Like a sphinx?

DIANA. Racks...on racks on racks.

GUS. Uhhhhh...

DIANA. You must make a way. You must blaze your own trail! You must take what's on the inside and put it on the outside!

GUS. Take what's inside and put it on the outside?

DIANA. Yes my son!

GUS. YES! That's brilliant! Yes! Thank you Saint Diana!

DIANA. No need to thank me...I am your patron. Your saint. I am your Inner Diva. I am the woman you always wanted to be! I. AM. DIANA. (*Sings, chant-like.*) In Duuuuboisian Liberace, In Homobus Carnitas. Gaaaaaaaaaymaaaaaaaaan.

　　　　Diana disappears.

GUS. Wait. Where are you going? Wait. How do I...?

　　　　Gus is transfixed. Tanner reappears.

TANNER. Gus!

GUS. (*Sings.*) I'M COMING OUT!

TANNER. Again?

GUS. The muse has descended! It's all in me baby!

TANNER. Yes it is! See! Great. You're so good!

GUS. Saaaaay, what was that play you took me to a while back. Office comedy. It was like in someone's basement.

TANNER. The Forum is not a basement. It's a totally respectable—

> *Gus kisses Tanner to silence him.*

GUS. —Yes—of course—you're so right. Who was the actress that played the secretary?

TANNER. Oh Vanessa from my improv class! God, I love her!

GUS. What's not to love right. You're in an improv class?

TANNER. …Yes…

GUS. Right.…

> *They stand in awkward silence.*

Can you put me in touch with her?

TANNER. Why?

GUS. It's a surprise?! Please?

TANNER. Sure. Uh… Let me find her number.

> *Tanner exits.*

4.

> *Vanessa and Gus in Gus' studio. Vanessa is as all American as they come. Gus is reading an audition with Vanessa. He is playing "J-Tip." Not an actor but truthful. [Please no "black guy voices."] Vanessa is playing "Erica."*

GUS. *(As J-Tip.)* What the hell you mean you done killed my baby?

VANESSA. *(As Erica. A better actor.)* I did what I had to do J.

GUS. Uh…

VANESSA. What?

GUS. I…I don't feel comfortable saying that word.

VANESSA. What word?

GUS. This one.

VANESSA. Oh.

GUS. Yeah.

VANESSA. Just…substitute it with something you feel comfortable saying.

GUS. Right.

(As J-Tip.) All my "colleagues" 'round here, talking shit about me, like I ain't a man.

VANESSA. Colleagues?

GUS. It's the same thing, right?

VANESSA. It's not—Never mind. You have more.

GUS. Oh right.

(As J-Tip.) You makin' the whole hood think I ain't a man!

VANESSA. (As Erica.) You ain't!

GUS. (As J-Tip.) I takes care of my fuckin' kids Erica!

VANESSA. (As Erica.) You supposed to! You got kids! You supposed to take care of 'em. I have spent my whole life taking care of kids. My momma had me when she was 15 years old and as soon as I was old enough I was the momma in the house! She was in the streets again. *I* wiped the noses. *I* changed the diapers. *I* walked the kids to the bus. All that, before I could go to school. I have a chance here to become somebody and this baby was all up in my way. I had to do it for me. It was my choice! You don't get to tell me what to do with my body, J-Tip!

(As Vanessa.) Scene. I don't actually say scene at the end of an audition…it's…my acting teacher just…never mind.

GUS. Wow.

VANESSA. What?

GUS. You're really really good.

VANESSA. Thank you.

GUS. What's this from? A play?

VANESSA. Musical.

GUS. I see. Tanner is a such a big fan of yours! I'm glad he could put us in touch.

VANESSA. Me too! He's really funny. He said you were working on an art project of some kind.

GUS. Yes!

VANESSA. What kind of art do you make?

GUS. Mostly painting. I've done some work that is collage but it always comes back to painting.

VANESSA. Nice.

GUS. Color is my place of inquiry.

VANESSA. I don't have much experience with art. I used to draw some, when I was little.

GUS. No experience required.

VANESSA. What do you want me to do?

GUS. What do you think of this piece of art? Do you like it?

    Vanessa looks at the painting Gus showed Jane earlier.

VANESSA. Okay.

…

…

…

Well

…

…

…

Huh…

    She tilts her head to the left.

Hmm…

…

…

    Then the right. She begins to nod. She's seeing it…[not really]

Huh…

…

…

…

Okay.

    Gus watches her.

GUS. It's something isn't it.

VANESSA. …well…

GUS. What?

VANESSA. I…

GUS. Say it.

VANESSA. It's a little…boring actually.

GUS. That's the desired effect.

VANESSA. What does it mean?

GUS. Mean?

VANESSA. I don't get it. It's just… It looks like…

GUS. Yes?

VANESSA. It's just blank…

GUS. There is a lot going on in this painting. It has volume and mass…but not just that… It's open. It's presenting itself to you as a mirror almost. You apply to the canvas, to the white paint, what you are. Who you are. You are the missing part of the art-making process.

VANESSA. Oh…well…I um…

GUS. Just… Look closer. Extend yourself into the world of the painting. Into the whiteness.

VANESSA. The whiteness… Alright.

She steps in.

GUS. Now. Step back.

VANESSA. Okay—

GUS. —Maybe? Anything?

VANESSA. I'll keep looking. So…why do you need an actress.

GUS. I want you to play an artist. To act the part of an artist.

VANESSA. Ohhhhhhhhh. This is like a performance art thing.

GUS. No. I need you to be the artist that painted this painting.

VANESSA. But you painted it, right?

GUS. Yes.

VANESSA. Why would you want someone else to take credit for your work?

GUS. It's complicated.

VANESSA. Give me the Reader's Digest.

GUS. I can't get into the Parnell Museum of Contemporary American Art.

VANESSA. Why?

GUS. 'Cause I'm a white man.

VANESSA. I see.

GUS. But you can.

VANESSA. I can?

GUS. 'Cause you're a black woman!

VANESSA. That is perfect irony.

GUS. I need you to become...a black artist for me. Together we can revolutionize the way people think about diversity.

VANESSA. I'm not really the revolutionary type.

GUS. You're an actress. A really talented actress I might add.

VANESSA. Thank you but—

GUS. —You can do anything. I will walk you through everything you need to know.

VANESSA. Don't you want people to recognize you for what you've created?

GUS. It's an exercise in absence. If I remove myself from the art...does it become something else? Do I become something else? You know?

VANESSA. No.

GUS. They aren't interested in white male artists.

VANESSA. Why should they be?

GUS. They don't want me! I'm going to give them what they want. I'm making a point. I'm trying to...prove something.

VANESSA. What?

GUS. To show them that...when you pick someone because of their race...you know...you may not be getting the best work...you limit what you have access to... It doesn't even matter if the art is good so long as the artist is right. Right? I hate that. It puts me on the edge. Why is it racism when it happens to someone black but if it's a white guy being discriminated against it's, I don't know, payback? And I know! I'm not supposed to say things like that but...That's how I feel. You know. I can't speak my truth. 'Cause to be a white man in America right now means you are rendered silent. How is that helping anything? What about my marginalization? I know. I know. You're giving me the silly-white-guy look. I'm going to say how I feel. I'm not going to be silent anymore! We are supposed to be so quiet. But that's over!

VANESSA. …So…uh…what you're saying is…and let me make sure I have this right… White men don't talk?

GUS. No, I'm not saying… It's bigger than that. You're not thinking about the bigger problem.

VANESSA. You know…that really scares me. Whenever I hear white folks say things like "the bigger problem." I think…what the hell is this secret "bigger problem"? Who knows! The white folks, apparently! And honestly… This is counter to my ambition. You know? Like, people need to know me. Vanessa.

GUS. Right.

> *Beat.*

You're right. You were great in the play we saw you in. What was it called again?

VANESSA. *All In a Day.* I was Shaundalisa.

GUS. Right right right. Tanner drags me to so many plays. They start to blur. You were very funny in that.

VANESSA. Thank you.

GUS. *(Laughing at the memory of the play.)* You had this…uh… monologue, at the beginning of the play when you first meet the lead. Jesus it was funny. You did this things where you—

VANESSA. —Wait. Let me see if I can—
(Channeling Shaundalisa.) Since you're new, I feel the need to give you some advice. First: I'm the receptionist. R. E. C. E. P. T. *(Thinks. Right.)* I. O. N. I. S. T. Receptionist. I receive. I am a professional receiver. I receive for a living. Mmmkay? I don't get coffee, I don't pick up dry cleaning. I don't do favors. I don't give, I receive. So don't try it. Failure is certain. Second: Friday is casual day. Don't try to go against the grain coming up in here in a suit on Friday. Don't. Do it. 'Cause I will be in my leopard print, velour sweatsuit with the pink accents and I don't want no trouble.

VANESSA and GUS. Don't start none, won't be none. We clear on that.

> *They do the two finger "We understand each other" gesture.*

24

GUS. I loved her!

VANESSA. Me too.

GUS. I felt really connected to her.

VANESSA. Yeah? How so?

GUS. You knooooooow. Every gay man has a black woman inside of him. Just dying to get out.

> *Silence. In the silence, Gus feels: "Am I right?" Vanessa feels: "Child please."*

VANESSA. Do you really believe that?

GUS. Oh no you didn't girlfriend! Honey Boom! Yeah, child! You'ain't know dat?! Don't get me all twisted up in here.

VANESSA. Have you ever met a black woman…you know…in like, real life that talks like that?

GUS. I'm sure I have.

VANESSA. I see.

GUS. That's why I think this matters so much. My work is really interrogating my own interiority. But having you present my work, I'm being more true to myself by exposing my inner self through you. Creating a real life version of…the black woman inside me. To be enjoyed by all. I want her voice to be heard. I want to create her with you.

VANESSA. Oh my god. I just read an article about this in the *Atlantic*. What did they call it? Uhph—Racial Tourism! That's it!

GUS. That's a new one.

VANESSA. No it's like…"Let me play double-dutch with the black girls on the playground 'cause they make me feel all empowered and fierce. They can teach me fun comebacks and how to wag my finger and I can be just as fierce and fabulous as them but, without the burden of actually being a black girl." I got that right?

GUS. Whoa…You don't know me.

VANESSA. I don't.

GUS. I'm not a racist.

VANESSA. This is really awkward for you.

GUS. I resent you saying that I am.

VANESSA. Did I say you were racist?

GUS. You implied it.

VANESSA. Implied?

GUS. Yes you—

VANESSA. —Did the words, Gus, You, Are, or Racist come out my mouth.

GUS. No.

VANESSA. So…

GUS. I just felt that I needed to make that…clear.

VANESSA. Why?

> *Silence.*

Uh huh. 'Cause you know it's questionable at the very least.

> *Vanessa starts gathering her belongings to leave.*

GUS. Wait. Don't go.

VANESSA. Look…I don't think I'm what you're looking for. It's no big deal. No harm. No foul.

GUS. You are what I'm looking for! This could be something we create together.

VANESSA. Why would I want to create a fake black woman with you?

GUS. 'Cause she could make you a household name.

VANESSA. What are you talking about man?

GUS. Can you imagine…undermining the entire visual art machine? Can you imagine exposing the hypocrisy of that museum? If we can get into this show on a lie…what does that say about the show.
Everyone would be talking about us. Everyone would know our names. Your name. I can make you famous. You could be the next Marina Abramović. I can make that happen for you.

VANESSA. I'm late for another audition.

GUS. Right.

…

Right.

…

Of course. You should think about it.

VANESSA. I will. Thank you.

Vanessa leaves. Gus sits.

5.

Gus and Tanner's apartment. They are in the midst of a lovely little make out moment. Perhaps shirts are off. It's definitely moving towards sexy time but not quite there yet.

TANNER. Oh God! Yes. Right there.

GUS. Mmmhmm

TANNER. Fuck.

GUS. Mmmhmm

TANNER. Wait…a little to the—

GUS. —Uh huh—

TANNER. —Yes yes. That's…uhhhhhhhh…Gus.

GUS. Do you think of me as a white man?

TANNER. What?

GUS. Do you think of me as a white man?

TANNER. Yes. Mmmmm.

GUS. You do?!

TANNER. Yeah. Wait…My foot's falling asleep. Oof. Thank you. Okay, kiss me.

GUS. I don't think of you as Asian.

TANNER. That's very modern of you.

GUS. I don't see you as different. I don't really see color.

TANNER. Good for you?

GUS. Well…I mean. Should I?

TANNER. I'd like to think, you see me as Tanner.

GUS. Right. Which is inclusive of your being Asian.

TANNER. Can we talk about this when we're not engaged in—

GUS. —Oh right right right right. I'm sorry.

They go back to the make-out. It's a good one.

TANNER. Mmhmm Mmhmm. Oh yeah. Uh huh. Ow. Not so—

GUS. —Better.

TANNER. Yes. Mmmmmmmmm Yeeeeeee/eeeees

GUS. / Just one more question. Do you hide things from me?

TANNER. What?

GUS. Like…like how you feel about politics or…or society?

TANNER. I don't think I do.

GUS. Sometimes you feel far away.

TANNER. I do?

GUS. Not totally. Maybe a little bit.

TANNER. Gus, I share everything with you.

GUS. Everything?

TANNER. Yes. My opinion. My finances. I'm currently trying to share my…gingerbread with you…

GUS. You're—Oh right.

TANNER. I think we have a very open and intimate relationship.

GUS. I do too. Things are good, right?

TANNER. Yes. Very good.

GUS. Good.

TANNER. Could you do me, now!

GUS. Oh yeah. I'm going to totally do you.

TANNER. Well let's go!

The make-out starts again. It's getting hotter. Gus is having a gold star evening.

Oh Gus…

GUS. Yes…

TANNER. Gus Eugene McKnight!

GUS. Yes…

TANNER. Don't stop…

GUS. Mmm Mmmhmmm…say…do you think I'm a racial tourist?

TANNER. What in the world is a racial tourist?

GUS. Like I want to experience other cultures as, like, novelties. Without the real difficulty of being a part of the culture.

TANNER. Oooooh Baby! You wouldn't last a day touring another race. You like to get your way too much.

GUS. So you think I am?

TANNER. No. Not necessarily.

GUS. But a little bit?

TANNER. No. Gus. Do you think I am?

GUS. You've only dated white men.

TANNER. Uh...no...I don't think that's true.

GUS. Every ex you've talked about was white.

TANNER. How do you know?

GUS. Like, how you described them.

TANNER. How do I describe them?

GUS. Like...the one...you know the one...when we first met you wouldn't shut up about him. He...uh...oh right he was like a famous botanist. You said he was like super conservative and that he only wore Brooks Brothers and he only listened to alt-rock. That's a white guy.

TANNER. Nelson?! You're talking about Nelson.

GUS. That's him! That guy!

TANNER. He's Haitian.

GUS. Well...he...he sounded—

TANNER. —Great! Now I'm flaccid.

GUS. I am NOT a racial tourist.

TANNER. Why are we half-naked talking about...racial tourism?! Gus! You sound like a crazy person.

GUS. Now I'm crazy!

TANNER. Yeah.

GUS. That's productive.

TANNER. We were having...or I was having a really lovely evening and now you are doing this thing that I don't understand. What is going on with you? You're bringing up my old boyfriends. What's up?

GUS. I just think we should talk about our...you know...racial sexual history.

TANNER. HUH?

GUS. It's what people do Tanner!

TANNER. No it's not! No one sits around talking about how many nationalities they've screwed.

GUS. Well I'm talking more in terms of race...I mean of course race falls along national lines but—

TANNER. —I'MDONEWITHTHIS!

GUS. You don't have to yell.

TANNER. No, I do. I've got three glasses of wine in me, I'm wearing the special underwear! Things are all...tidy down there and my hormones are raging. The last thing I want to talk about are the fucking politics of interracial dating. Stop being such a puddle!

GUS. A puddle.

TANNER. Just wet and muddy and something people avoid.

GUS. That was very literary.

> Tanner begins to exit.

We're talking! Where are you going?

TANNER. To wack off in the shower.

6.

> In the studio. Gus works on a painting. Vanessa enters.
>
> [Over the course of this scene multiple days pass. I suggest very little costume changes, if any. Perhaps they both wear artist smocks of some kind that allow time to be fluid? I don't know. Figure it out.]

VANESSA. You sure do love white.

GUS. Oh! Hey! How did you—

VANESSA. I slipped in while someone was leaving.

GUS. You're back.

VANESSA. Yeah.

GUS. Why?

VANESSA. I want to be famous.

GUS. Yeah?

VANESSA. I want people to look at me.

GUS. Join the club.

VANESSA. I want to make a version of me that people can't ignore. To be...visible.

GUS. I know the feeling.

VANESSA. What scares you?

GUS. Losing control.

VANESSA. Had that answer ready didn't you?

GUS. It keeps me up at night.

VANESSA. I'm going to do this with you.

GUS. Oh my god that's great.

VANESSA. We make this...*Together.*

GUS. Sure.

VANESSA. I want to be involved in all of the choices.

GUS. Of course. 100% Collaboration.

VANESSA. I don't want any funny business. I know you think you're funny and all, but I'm serious about this.

GUS. Scout's Honor.

> *Beat.*

Do we have a deal?

VANESSA. We've got a deal.

GUS. Yes?

VANESSA. Yes.

GUS. YAAAAAS!

VANESSA. Boy please. Soooo...What would I get?

GUS. There's a stipend.

VANESSA. No. I mean...what do I get out of this?

GUS. What do you want?

VANESSA. I don't know.

GUS. It's worse when you do know.

Next day.

VANESSA. —What should we name her?

GUS. You. What should we name you?

VANESSA. Sure.

GUS. I was thinking something like Simone.

VANESSA. I always wanted a name like that when I was growing up. Something…normal.

GUS. Can't get more normal than Vanessa.

VANESSA. It's not my real name.

GUS. Oh! What's your real name?

VANESSA. VanKneesia. The K is silent.

GUS. …Oh…

VANESSA. My mother gave us all names that sounded very…

GUS. What?

VANESSA. Urban. I changed it to Vanessa when I was in school. Sounded more cosmopolitan.

GUS. Wow. You hated the name that much?

VANESSA. Oh yeah. My family has insane names. I have two cousins back home named Cradenzanique and Albenaesha. They're twins fraternal.

GUS. That's rough.

VANESSA. Yeah. What about something like that. A crazy name. Like…Balkonaé.

GUS. What?!

VANESSA. It's so good! Balkonaé…Townsend.

GUS. Oh my god. That's…That's…

VANESSA. What?

GUS. Brilliant! You're brilliant!

VANESSA. Okay! Great! This is fun!

GUS. I told you we would make a great team.

Day five.

VANESSA. So…How old am I?

GUS. You're 31.

VANESSA. Right on.

GUS. And you're a lesbian.

VANESSA. Okay.

GUS. And you're colorblind.

VANESSA. That explains a lot about these paintings.

GUS. You went to Yale.

VANESSA. Majored in…?

GUS. African American Studies and Art.

VANESSA. Alright. Family?

GUS. Of course.

Beat.

Your father was a—

VANESSA. —Yes?

GUS. What do you think?

VANESSA. A bus driver.

GUS. I like that. I was thinking your mother should be a care-giver. A nurse?

VANESSA. Hospice Nurse.

GUS. Nice. You have one sibling, a sister. Her name is Sarah. You're / the youngest.

VANESSA. / Sarah? No…needs more syllables.

GUS. Why?

VANESSA. No mother names one child Sarah and the next Balkonaé. Alright. You want people to believe this right? Listen to the real black woman. Not the one prancing around in your head. Her name is… Destinatosha.

GUS. Sure. Sure.

VANESSA. Private or public school?

GUS. I think private. A liberal school. Like a Quaker School. Not Catholic. Too rigid.

VANESSA. Alright. Studied cello and piano starting at age 9.

GUS. You and your sister.

VANESSA. Sister is a concert pianist. She lives in Berlin with her husband and their two children. Cute little caramel-colored boys with curly blond hair and brown eyes that call me on the phone on Sundays.

GUS. I love the specificity of that.

VANESSA. When do you think I read *Their Eyes Were Watching God*?

GUS. Oh. I hadn't thought about…is that a must?

VANESSA. *(Firmly.)* Yes.

GUS. 19.

VANESSA. 15.

GUS. Okay. You began working in my studio about two years ago. During the last year of a residency.

VANESSA. Perfect. I speak three languages.

GUS. English, French, and—

VANESSA. Farsi.

GUS. Your parents retired to Georgia. They wanted to return to their roots. You spent a year studying in Greece and did a fellowship in Iceland.

VANESSA. And…I created installations in Australia.

GUS. Budapest.

VANESSA. Cambodia and…

GUS. Kenya.

VANESSA. That's good.

> *Day eight.*

GUS. Your favorite show growing up was *The Cosby Show*.

VANESSA. Oh! Okay. That's…novel.

GUS. It just makes sense. Right?

VANESSA. Well. Yeah. Sure. I mean…everybody wanted to be a Huxtable! I thought my family was the Huxtables, then I realize…

nope…we're kinda poor. HA!!! There is this episode called "Off to See the Wretched."

GUS. The what?

VANESSA. The Wretched.

GUS. As in "of the earth"?

VANESSA. No. It's Vanessa's favorite band.

GUS. Wait did you name yourself after a Cosby Kid?

VANESSA. …Maybe…Whatever. Anyway. Don't you remember that episode?

GUS. No.

VANESSA. Oh! It's the best!

GUS. I see.

VANESSA. So Vanessa and her friends are going to see this band and she lies to Claire and Cliff—

GUS. —Who's Cliff?

VANESSA. Cliff.

> *Beat.*

Cliff Huxtable. The dad.

GUS. Wait. I thought Bill Cosby was the dad?

VANESSA. Huh?

GUS. Wasn't—

VANESSA. —Oh! Well yeah. It's okay people always confuse Bill Cosby with Heathcliff Huxtable but they are soooo different. Bill Cosby played the dad…but he…the character was Heathcliff Huxtable.

GUS. …Really?

> *Silence. Vanessa just sort of looks at Gus.*

VANESSA. Anyway… So Vanessa tells them she is staying at a friend's house and they are going to see the Wretched in New York. But they are actually off / to…

GUS. / To see the Wretched /

VANESSA. / In Baltimore.

GUS. This was a long episode.

VANESSA. You know what...never mind. We don't need to go through—

GUS. —What's the big deal?! They are going to a concert. So what?!

VANESSA. The big deal is the concert is in Baltimore. They are in New York, and you're not supposed to lie to your mother.

GUS. I lied to my mother all the time.

VANESSA. ...There's a joke in there somewhere...

GUS. So...they go to the concert, and...

VANESSA. ...and Kara's brother's car—

GUS. —Jesus! Who's Kara?

VANESSA. Would you please—

GUS. —Fine. Kara's brother.

VANESSA. Kara's brother's *car* gets stolen in Wilmington.

GUS. Delaware?

VANESSA. Yes.

GUS. Got it.

VANESSA. Meanwhile...Claire finds out that the Wretched aren't performing in New York but in Baltimore.

GUS. Uh oh.

VANESSA. I know right!

GUS. Was this a to-be-continued episode?

VANESSA. So they have to go pick up Vanessa and bring her home from Baltimore. Now when they get home, Claire goes off on her. Whew! She keeps saying "Big FUN! BIIIIIG FUN." Over and over again. It's really funny. Oh and Claire keeps asking Vanessa questions right, and every time Vanessa tries to speak Claire says "SHUT. UP. Don't you dare open your mouth when I'm asking you a question." Theeeeeen Claire says "You went all the way to Baltimore. Maryland. With the Wretched to have BIIIIIG Fun! What else did you have in Baltimore, Vanessa, well let's see...you had donuts. Tell me...So how is it, Vanessa, that you didn't get in to *see* the Wretched and have the big fun." So by now Vanessa is too scared to speak... Claire waits and then says... "You better answer me when I'm asking you a question, girl."

Vanessa peals into laughter. Gus just watches.

It's funny, right?

GUS. Ha…

VANESSA. That's my favorite episode.

GUS. I'm sorry. I don't get it.

VANESSA. What's not to get? Claire. Goes. Off!

> *Silence.*

Let's talk about the costume.

GUS. Oooookay.

> *Gus produces several costume pieces. He arranges them on
> the floor for Vanessa to inspect. Vanessa walks around and
> takes the costume in. It is all very "Black Hipster Chic." [Note:
> This is a very real neo-stereotype of the black female body.
> Google: Solange Knowles.]*

VANESSA. It's a lot.

GUS. You think?

VANESSA. Yes.

GUS. I like it.

VANESSA. This is…I don't know. A bit on the nose. It's sort of cliché.

GUS. We are invading the stereotype in order to destroy it.

VANESSA. We? I'm the one that has to wear it. And this wig…

GUS. It's a good wig.

> *Beat.*

Right?

VANESSA. 'Cause you wear so many wigs and you know what a
good wig is?

GUS. Fine. We can augment the costume.

VANESSA. That's all I wanted. I'm not hard to please.

> *Day fifteen.*

GUS. Did you read the artist statement I wrote for you?

VANESSA. Yes.

GUS. Awesome!

VANESSA. I would like to suggest a few changes.

GUS. Changes?

VANESSA. To the content.

GUS. What content?

VANESSA. Well I felt like I would have more to say about my mother as an influence.

GUS. Why?

VANESSA. She taught me to draw. She gave me my first paints. She took me to my first museum. I'm not seeing why this is a problem.

GUS. It's not a problem. I just want to know what's going on so I can...you know...support you. That's all.

  Beat.

So I have an idea.

VANESSA. Yes?

GUS. How about a little roleplay? Huh?! Huh?! Great idea right?!

VANESSA. Alllllright.

GUS. So I'm going to be Jane. I'm gonna ask you a few questions and you answer as Balkonaé.

VANESSA. Are you Jane now?

GUS. What? Oh...well no.
(As Jane.) Now I am.

VANESSA. I can't really tell...when you're like...I mean...I need to believe—

GUS. —Alright fine.
(As Jane.) Balkonaé! Dear it's soooooo nice to meet you!

VANESSA. You too! It is such a huuuuuuge honor to get to meet the illustrious Jane Foooooooorsyyyyyyyyyyth!

GUS. What's that?

VANESSA. What's what?

GUS. That's not Balkonaé!

VANESSA. Excuse me?

GUS. Her voice is more centered. More earthy. More...

VANESSA. How do you know?

38

GUS. She—

VANESSA. Me!

GUS. Yes! You! I want you to be more grounded. More…

Vanessa tries out different voice placements.

VANESSA. My art is an extension of my experience—

GUS. —No.

VANESSA. Alright
(Another.) When I first started to work with Gus I was—

GUS. —Oh God no!

VANESSA. You just gonna cut me off like…alright…How about…
(Eartha Kitt? Maybe?) Theeeeeee puuuuuuurpose of my use of the coloooooor white. Is too—

GUS. —No!

VANESSA. *(Nails it. Earthy. Soulful.)* Look, I don't know what to tell you man!

GUS. That's it!

VANESSA. Yeah? Like that?

GUS. Yes! Okay, now I'm Jane.
(As Jane.) Balkonaé. Tell me a little bit about this work?

VANESSA. Well…I was on a spiritual retreat in India and it all came to me one evening. It was severely hot and I may have been hallucinating a touch…but I saw this sea of emptiness. A vast ocean of absence, I want to capture that here.

GUS. *(As Jane.)* I just love that. You are a really exciting voice.

VANESSA. Aw man. Thanks.

GUS. Talk to me about what inspires you.

VANESSA. My vagina.

GUS. What? That's a little crass.

VANESSA. Just 'cause you don't like them doesn't make them bad.

GUS. Did I say that?! Jane will be here tomorrow and you are deliberately antagonizing me.

VANESSA. I am not. I'm trying to figure her out!

GUS. I already figured her out!

VANESSA. Ohhhhhh. Have you?

GUS. I mean… You know what I meant?

VANESSA. I knew this was a bad idea.

GUS. Oh come on. I…I just want it to be right?

VANESSA. Do you trust me?

GUS. Yes!

VANESSA. No really! Do you?

GUS. Yes. I do.

VANESSA. Then let me do what I do.

GUS. Alright. Fine.
(As Jane.) So…your vagina.

VANESSA. And my mother.

GUS. *(As Jane.)* Lovely.
(As Gus.) Excellent.

> *Day twenty.*

VANESSA. Am I on social media?

GUS. What like…Twitter?

VANESSA. Yeah. Could be a good way to…solidify her persona.

GUS. Right. Good call.

VANESSA. Remember Myspace. I had…a Myspace account. In college. It was this totally created version of me. Pictures of me in wigs with sunglasses. Quoting writers and emo songs. I wanted to not be me. Think that's a part of why I became an actor. I get to be everybody. Anyway. I had this account of this person I created. It was me, sort of, but it wasn't, you know?

GUS. Yeah.

VANESSA. I used my own name and age and it was a version of me in those pictures but it was truly an experiment in becoming someone else. I think Facebook came out. Not long after. But that Myspace page is still out there. Still telling the universe that I am really into French films and how much I cried when I found out Elliott Smith was dead. That version is there for anyone. Like a fossil. One day there will be all of the versions of me floating on the… wherever things like that go when we are done being that person.

She walks closer to the painting. She stares at it for a great long while.

GUS. Hey. You okay?

Vanessa keeps staring at the painting.

We can...end for the day if you're tired.

Vanessa keeps staring.

Vanessa.

VANESSA. I think I'm vegan.

7.

Gus' studio. Jane enters. Jane looks at Gus. Gus looks at Jane.

GUS. Thank you for coming.

JANE. Hey...I hope there are no hard feelings.

GUS. Not at all. Water under the bridge.

JANE. Oh Good! I was afraid you were gonna try to convince me to put you in the show again.

GUS. What? NO! Pah!

JANE. Well good!

GUS. I do want you to meet someone really special.

JANE. Okay.

GUS. I have discovered the most remarkable young artist.

JANE. Have you?

GUS. Just look at this work!

JANE. This one?

GUS. Incredible right?

JANE. It's quite good. It's very much in the vein of your work actually.

GUS. It's not mine. It's by a woman!

JANE. It is?

GUS. A Blaaaaaa-frican American woman.

> [So, a note on this: Blaaaaa-frican American—He is negoti-
> ating, in the very moment, what to call this imagined woman.
> He starts to say black but decides instead to say African
> American and mistakenly blurs them. Thus creating a new
> "ethnicity" for her. Let it be as stupid as possible.]

JANE. …A…Blaaaa-frican American woman?

> Gus: Aww hell, just go with it.

GUS. Yep. That's uh…how, she identifies…ethnically.

JANE. Ethnically?

GUS. Yeah.

JANE. Huh.

GUS. And she's a lesbian.

JANE. Oh I love that! That's good.

GUS. And colorblind.

JANE. No!

GUS. Yes!

JANE. Shut up!

GUS. I won't!

JANE. What's her name?

GUS. It's Balkonaé…

JANE. Balcony?

GUS. No…uh…Balkonaé…Townsend.

JANE. Spell that?

GUS. B. A. L. K. O. N. A. E. Accent aigu.

JANE. Huh. Clever.

GUS. Want to meet her?

JANE. Suuuuure.

GUS. She's just in the back cleaning some brushes. *(Calling off.)*
Balkonaé

BALKONAÉ. *(Offstage.)* WHAT!

GUS. *(Calling off.)* Jane is here.

BALKONAÉ. Aight hold up.

> *Balkonaé enters. Fierce! Amazing! The costume, the hair, the shoes. She's a fricking vision! Jane is sort of stunned by her.*

JANE. Oh My!

GUS. Jane…this…is Balkonaé Townsend.

BALKONAÉ. Sup.

JANE. Hello Ba…Bal…uh…

BALKONAÉ. Balkonaé.

JANE. Yes. Right. I'm Jane Forsyth. I'm head curator at—

BALKONAÉ. —There is a dark aura in here. Something's clouding my focus.

JANE. Oh. My. I hope I didn't bring in something from off the street. I'm very aware of these sorts of things. Auras and the like.

GUS. Uh… Balkonaé remember I told you that someone from the Parnell was coming by.

BALKONAÉ. Ooooooooooh yeeeeeah. Greetings. Welcome to my Studio.

GUS. Well actually—

JANE. —Gus please. *(To Balkonaé.)* Hello.

BALKONAÉ. Gus said you might like my work.

JANE. I do. Very much.

BALKONAÉ. What did you like about it?

JANE. It's honest.

BALKONAÉ. You think?

JANE. Yes.

BALKONAÉ. Well…thanks!

JANE. I would love to hear more about where you're coming from.

BALKONAÉ. Coming from?

JANE. Yes.

GUS. She calls her work…Bad Bitch Expressionism.

BALKONAÉ. Yup!

JANE. Bad Bitch Expressionism!

BALKONAÉ. Re-Appropriation of the negative, as foundational to the full expression of black femaleness.

JANE. I am in love with this woman.
Where did you come to this idea? This Bad Bitch Expressionism?

BALKONAÉ. Well you know. It's coming from my experience as a black woman.

JANE. You mean, Blafrican American. I just love that by the way.

GUS. Me too. So clever.

BALKONAÉ. Yeah, blafrican american. I dug the ring of that.

JANE. It's very organic.

BALKONAÉ. Au Naturale.

JANE. You knooooooow, when Gus and I were in college, I spent a year on an American Indian reservation. Remember that Gus?

GUS. You went on and on about it.

JANE. It was so eye-opening.

BALKONAÉ. Are you Native American?

JANE. An eighth.

BALKONAÉ. Wow.

JANE. It was one of the most important moments in my life. I felt... I had a more complete picture of who I am.

BALKONAÉ. Wow, that is...great.

JANE. Bad Bitch Expressionism! Just love that!

BALKONAÉ. Uh huh?

JANE. Yes. It's fascinating. Is it a response to the exclusivity you feel from mainstream feminism?

BALKONAÉ. Oh yeah.

JANE. I'm always having those conversations with my friends about how exclusive we can be. Intersectionality is important! What inspires your work?

BALKONAÉ. Uh...well you know.

JANE. I don't.

BALKONAÉ. I mean. Ladies like you.

JANE. Me?

BALKONAÉ. Yes Miss Lady! We are modern day deities. We are goddesses. Extraterrestrial.

JANE. Yes!

BALKONAÉ. So my work is a celebration of that. That sounds like you to me. You run stuff right?

JANE. Well, I depend on a lot of people. A whole team in fact—

BALKONAÉ. —Oh I get that, but for real…Who runs that place? It ain't the "team."

JANE. Well I do.

BALKONAÉ. Don't whisper that! Say "I RUN THIS!"

JANE. I RUN THIS!

BALKONAÉ. "I'MMA BOSS!"

JANE. I'MMA BOSS!

BALKONAÉ. That's it!

JANE. I see what you're saying!

BALKONAÉ. You're a woman that embraces her inner contradictions. Relishes in her imperfections. Her ugliness. Her loud and rude voice in a world that restricts her speech. The ownership of your flaws and the celebration of your beauty even when it's not beautiful. Like those earring you're wearing.

GUS. Uh—

JANE. —I love these earrings!

GUS. They're great earrings!

BALKONAÉ. And you should love them. They ugly as sin, but they yours. You know what I mean. You wear those god awful things with pride! 'Cause yuh can! You pickin' up what I'm layin' down?

JANE. Oh yes! Yes! Right on sister!

BALKONAÉ. Whoop dere it is!

JANE. My my my you are so eloquent about the ideas.

BALKONAÉ. I speak well too don't I?

JANE. Yes!

BALKONAÉ. I mean fundamentally…I'm attempting to acquire privilege as a woman, a blaaaaafrican american woman, and a queer

45

woman. I do that by using the master narrative and turning it inside out to reveal its ugliness. In essence, by exposing my own ugliness. It's my obligation as a successful artist to make people aware of their own racism and patriarchy and misogyny.

JANE. I like you.

BALKONAÉ. Of course you do! I'm a damn delight!

JANE. *(Laughs a bit.)* You aaaaaare. Well. I'm very interested. I really want to follow your career.

BALKONAÉ. You serious?

JANE. Yes!

BALKONAÉ. She serious?

GUS. Very.

BALKONAÉ. Deadass?

JANE. Not sure I know how to respond to that.

BALKONAÉ. You seem bout your business. Real sharp!

JANE. You are just a treat.

BALKONAÉ. You hear that Gus? A treat.

GUS. Treat.

BALKONAÉ. Like a Brownie!

GUS. I'm so glad I could bring you two together!

BALKONAÉ. Yeah Gus! You a regular Christopher Columbus. Bumping into shit by mistake and claiming it for the queen.

GUS. Ha. Hahahahahahahahaha.

JANE. Oh my look at the time! I have to go. Ms. Townsend, I'll be in touch. Gus, you're a doll. So excited.

BALKONAÉ. Me too girlfriend.

Jane exits. Gus and Vanessa celebrate.

GUS. We did it!

VANESSA. Yes! We did!

GUS. We are in there! How did that feel?

VANESSA. She felt soooooooo good Gus! She's everything I wish I could be. You know? I'm so buttoned up but Balkonaé. She feels so…right! It's like what's on the inside is on the outside now.

46

GUS. Oh. I see. Okay—

VANESSA. —Like this woman has always been there. And we have unleashed her! Sexy and unruly and womanish.

GUS. Uh huh. Great.

Vanessa removes her wig.

VANESSA. Uh! She made me soooooo supremely aware of my butt and my belly. I always try to bind these parts of my body into submission but…when I'm her…I'm in love with my fat ass and my round belly. I'm in love with how big I am! I have some ideas about how we can implement those feelings into the paintings.

GUS. Sure. I mean. My work isn't really about that but—

VANESSA. Oh I know. But I think it could be good to connect the talking points with the experience of the art. I was thinking you could make a few of the pieces interactive… Maybe like a scratch and sniff situation? What you think?—

GUS. Scratch and sniff—

JANE. *(From offstage.)* —Oh Gus! I had another thought.

GUS. Quick wig!

Vanessa replaces the wig on her head just as Jane enters.

JANE. I just had an amazing idea! Ms. Townsend is New America!! What if I included Ms. Townsend in the New America Exhibition!

GUS. REALLY?!

JANE. Yes! I think she is perfect!

GUS. I agree.

JANE. I think that is the best way to introduce Bal…Ms. Townsend. I wanna shake things up! *(To Balkonaé.)* Could you select six pieces for the show?

GUS. SIX!?!

JANE. Yes. I'll have my assistant Zivia pick them up by the end of the week.

GUS. Oh…Uh…Well…That's not possible…

JANE. No? Why not?

BALKONAÉ. Well you see, I…uh…

GUS. Well…I mean…I don't want to speak for Balkonaé…

JANE. Seems like you are.

BALKONAÉ. You know what!!!! I can do it!

GUS. You can? You Can!

JANE. Yes?!

BALKONAÉ. I would be delighted Miss Lady.

GUS. YAY!

BALKONAÉ. Mmhmmm!

JANE. Well I have to go. So wonderful to meet you Bal…Oh dear. I just don't want to butcher your name.

BALKONAÉ. Oh…that's so sweet. Hey, tell…who composed *The Nutcracker.*

JANE. Tchaikovsky

BALKONAÉ. Oh that's right. And uuuuuuh who wrote *Crime and Punishment.*

JANE. Dostoyevsky.

BALKONAÉ. Uh huh. One more say "A Little Night Music" in German.

JANE. *(Like butter.) Eine kleine Nachtmusik.*

BALKONAÉ. Perfect! Say Balkonaé.

JANE. Balcony.

BALKONAÉ. Amazing.

JANE. I'm…Oh…I didn't mean to—

BALKONAÉ. —I'm just messing with you Miss Lady.

JANE. You can call me Jane.

BALKONAÉ. Such a refreshingly simple and uncomplicated name. Jane. Not much to it.

JANE. It's a family name.

BALKONAÉ. Probably goes back to the *Mayflower* doesn't it. Jane. Lovely. And you can call meeeeee… Say it with me now.

JANE. Baaaaaaah

BALKONAÉ. You'll get it. BAL.

JANE. BAL.

BALKONAÉ. CON.

JANE. CON.

BALKONAÉ. NAY.

JANE. NAY.

BALKONAÉ. BALKONAÉ.

JANE. BAL…

BALKONAÉ. BAL. CON. NAY.

JANE. BAL. CON. NAY.

BALKONAÉ. Come on Gus! You too! BAL. CON. NAY.

JANE and GUS. BAL. CON. NAY.

BALKONAÉ. Balkonaé!

JANE. Balcony!

BALKONAÉ. Close enough.

JANE. What does it mean?

BALKONAÉ. "A view from on high." Jazzy right?

JANE. Beautiful. This has certainly been fruitful! I could stay here all day but, alas, I have to go. It's great meeting you…Ms. Townsend. Gus, I'll see you soon.

BALKONAÉ. Take care Miss Lady.

GUS. Bye.

> *Jane exits.*

You went off script!

BALKONAÉ. I took some liberties, sure.

GUS. You promised her six pieces.

BALKONAÉ. You bet your sweet pink ass I did.

GUS. I only have the one! And that name game thing you played. How could you?

BALKONAÉ. Remember you told me I could be who I wanted? Remember?

GUS. You don't have any more work! Just this!

BALKONAÉ. Oh.

GUS. Yes!

BALKONAÉ. Well…I guess you should get to work!

GUS. Vanessa.

BALKONAÉ. Who?

GUS. You.

BALKONAÉ. Me?

GUS. Yes.

BALKONAÉ. Bitch where?

GUS. Vanessa, stop it.

BALKONAÉ. The fuck you talking about.

GUS. Whoa! That's a little aggressive.

BALKONAÉ. Did I hurt your feelings?

GUS. Vanessa, it's me. Gus.

BALKONAÉ. I'm glad you know who *you* are 'cause you damn sure don't know who *I* am.

GUS. You have majorly derailed the plan.

BALKONAÉ. The only plan I know about is how I'm bout to BLOW UUUUUUP.

GUS. Girl, you can't blow up without art.

BALKONAÉ. Au contrare sweet cheeks! You see all of this fine-ness standing here. I don't neeeeeeeeeeeeeeeeeed no white backdrops boo boo!

GUS. Hey. Listen. This…this thing has got to stay on track if I'm going to be able to make the statement I want to make. You can't go rogue.

BALKONAÉ. You think I give a fuck about your statement. I'm a statement. I'm a damn institution. Bitch look at this skin honey. CoCo Butter. That buttery shit! I ain't wuuuuuuuuuuurried bout your statement. I'm worried about this re-ven-nue bitch.

GUS. You're starting to make me feel a little uncomfortable.

BALKONAÉ. That's none of my business.

GUS. I created you!

BALKONAÉ. Fuck you!

GUS. What?

BALKONAÉ. You created me? Fuck you, you created me. Fuck outta here with that! Do you have any idea how offensive that is?

GUS. Whoa, wait…

BALKONAÉ. You tried it! You talking to me like you lost your mind!

GUS. Vanessa stop!

BALKONAÉ. You are so obsessed with this Vanessa chick! Look at me! Vanessa can't see me Gus! She's gone Gus! She ain't coming back! Might as well get used to me! 'Cause I'm here to stay.

GUS. But you *are* Vanesssa!

BALKONAÉ. Says who?

GUS. Says…you just are.

BALKONAÉ. Alright. Then I'm gonna start calling you Jack Spratt. How's that?

GUS. I think maybe we have taken this a little too far. Don't you think?

BALKONAÉ. No. I'm having the time of my life.

GUS. Okay look…we—

BALKONAÉ. —This ain't a conversation!

GUS. I don't want to do this anymore.

BALKONAÉ. Oh. You don't?

GUS. No! I don't.

BALKONAÉ. Well that's too bad girl. 'Cause it's happening and we are here.

GUS. Vanessa.

> *Balkonaé walks over to Gus and gets as close to his face as she can. It should feel as though she might kiss him.*

BALKONAÉ. You don't get it do you.

GUS. Get what?

BALKONAÉ. This…Vanessa, this art, your whack ass…this is all mine. Yes bitch…get into me!

8.

Gus and Tanner's apartment. Gus is feverishly trying to finish painting. He paints violently throughout this scene.

TANNER. I keep trying to convince myself that you are not actually a crazy person but that you just…I don't know…need to pretend to be a crazy person for what you do. Like you need to appear eccentric and provocative to be appealing but…there are these days where I think to myself, "No, he's insane and you should run." What the hell were you thinking?

GUS. I wasn't. It just got ahead of me.

TANNER. Jesus, Gus.

GUS. It's done now. I've done it and I really don't want you to make me feel worse. I'm making a point.

TANNER. Which is?

GUS. I'm not being judged by my merit! I'm being lumped into a demographic that doesn't even see me most of the time! I'm just another white man. No one is interested in my voice or anyone's voice for that matter. They're concerned with how the institution looks. Diversity numbers! "Are we diverse enough?! We don't need another white man on our walls."

TANNER. They're not and they don't. You've even said that, Gus.

GUS. Yes but—

TANNER. —This is something you've said to me. / Now, I was happy for you.

GUS. / And it was usually inclusive of my—

TANNER. …but this…this just seems—You're using her.

GUS. I'm not using her. / Would you please let me finish?

TANNER. / Yes you are. You are taking who she is / and

GUS. / I'm leveling the playing field. / I've worked my ass off.

TANNER. / Oh stop! You think you're the only artist that's / worked their ass off.

GUS. / I deserve to be in this show!

TANNER. Oh my god. Deserve?

GUS. *(Greek tragedy.)* Why is a white man in America demanding equal rights always seen as crazy!

TANNER. When we first started dating…I used to think…Am I the thing that makes him safe from scrutiny? Do I give him the magic card that will allow him to say things like "I'm not racist. I'm fucking the Asian guy!" But decided that you are not that person. / You're more evolved than that. But this gives me pause.

GUS. / Fucking the Asian guy. How can you stand here and say this to me. You think I've been using you?

TANNER. I don't know! I don't understand you right now. I think if you were a better artist you wouldn't need to do this.

GUS. That was hurtful.

TANNER. I meant it to be. I want to be mean to you right now, 'cause I don't know what to do with you right now. If you can steal a whole person that makes me wonder / what have you stolen from me maybe?

GUS. / You think I haven't been discriminated against? You think I don't know / what that feels like! I know.

TANNER. *(Mean.)* / Yes! I know you understand marginalization because someone called you faggot in the sixth grade before you even knew what the word meant and it just rocked your little world, right? I will never understand why people who have everything laid out before them want so desperately for the world to believe that they are being cheated. Get a fucking life Gus!

> *Beat.*

I'm sorry.

GUS. No you're not.

TANNER. Fine. I'm not sorry.

GUS. That is ugly.

TANNER. Congratulations on your "statement." I'm sure you'll end the epidemic of reverse racism.

GUS. You're not better than me Tanner.

TANNER. What?

GUS. Your experience doesn't give you the right to diminish mine.

TANNER. I'm not trying to diminishing you.

GUS. Yes you are!

TANNER. That's what you're taking away from this?

GUS. Yes.

TANNER. Gus...we live in a world that is designed to make sure that someone who looks like you can move smoothly. The artists in Jane's show...I'm willing to wager, haven't had the success you have, they probably ain't besties with the head curator. But you are. I've seen you struggle Gus. I live with you. I know the most intimate details of your pain. I feel it too. Sometimes I don't think you can feel other people's pain.

> *Tanner and Gus sit in silence. It's the harshest moment we have seen so far. Finally:*

GUS. When you look at me, what do you see?

TANNER. Someone I should know.

GUS. I see.

TANNER. What do you see when you look at me?

GUS. I see myself in you. I see me.

TANNER. You see yourself when you look at me.

GUS. Yes.

TANNER. I'm just a mirror.

GUS. I didn't say that. I just mean...we are no different. You're the same as me.

TANNER. We're different, Gus.

GUS. No we're.

TANNER. We are different.

GUS. I love you.

TANNER. Oh I know that. I feel that. But that's not what I'm talking about. I wanna know what causes you to fashion whoever you meet into your own image. I just don't know how to do that. That...is a superpower.

GUS. Don't you understand what I'm trying to do?

TANNER. No.

GUS. Right.

TANNER. You can't have everything you want.

GUS. I know that.

TANNER. No. You don't really.

GUS. Help me.

>   *Tanner kisses Gus.*

TANNER. That's all I can give you baby.

>   *Gus alone.*

GUS. Diana. Patron Saint of Wayward Gay Men.
Thrower of Shade. Reader of Men.
Diana. Diana. Diana!

>   *Diana, heavenly and divine, appears. Lofty. High above. She
>   sits in a slip of moonlight. Her halo brighter than before. She
>   looks down at Gus.*

DIANA. Son?

GUS. I'm here.

DIANA. I will never leave you or forsake you.

GUS. Give me the answer.

DIANA. You have the answer inside you.

GUS. I did that.

DIANA. That's not you.

GUS. It's not?

DIANA. No.

GUS. What do I do?

DIANA. I have been watching. I give no answers. I just bestow
fabulousness.

GUS. That's it?

DIANA. Go be fierce my child.

GUS. Go be fierce?

DIANA. Beautify and inspire wonder.

GUS. This is so phony.

DIANA. Multiply and sissify the world!

GUS. I don't know how.

DIANA. *(Becoming fed up.)* Fierceness comes from inside. If you have it, it shines.

GUS. It…

DIANA. Blessed are you my son. Go.

GUS. But—

DIANA. —Go—

GUS. —But—

DIANA. —Go! I can't give you anything else, honey!

GUS. But—

DIANA. —Go figure it out.

GUS. But you're supposed to—

DIANA. —Snap three times and say "there's no place like home."

GUS. That was a bit dismissive.

DIANA. That's 'cause I'm dismissing you!

GUS. Hey! You started this!

DIANA. Me?

GUS. Yes!

DIANA. You know what your problem is Gus. You don't listen.

GUS. I don't listen.

DIANA. No! Ya don't listen. I've been telling you from the beginning "look inside you" not hire somebody else to be you.

GUS. But—

DIANA. You can't fake fierce honey. The truth will come out.

GUS. I—I just wanted to prove something.

DIANA. Did you?

GUS. Did I what?

DIANA. Prove your point?

GUS. I don't know.

DIANA. Pitiful.

56

GUS. That's not necessary.

DIANA. You wanna know why I'm up here and you're down there?

GUS. Why?

DIANA. 'Cause I create. I don't imitate!

GUS. But it's my artwork.

DIANA. Then why does everyone think someone else did it?

GUS. You told me to tell them that!

DIANA. Nooooooo! *I* said the power was inside *you*!

GUS. But you're inside me.

DIANA. I'm up here.

GUS. And in me?

DIANA. Well honey I can't be two places at once.

GUS. Wait. You're not inside me?

DIANA. Can you not see me up here?

GUS. I'm so confused.

DIANA. You can look at a star. You can even enjoy its brightness. But you can never have its brilliance. It's light years away.

> *Beat. Beat. Beat.*

GUS. What's that even mean?

DIANA. Get your own light! And stop knocking on my dressing room door.

> *Diana disappears.*

9.

> *Sunrise the next morning. Gus sits and stares at his newest painting. Tanner enters.*

TANNER. It's good.

GUS. Oh. Hey.

TANNER. Did you sleep?

GUS. No.

TANNER. Me either.

GUS. Had to finish this.

TANNER. I'm about to head to work.

GUS. Uh huh.

TANNER. I said some things last night that…uh…

GUS. Me too.

TANNER. I hate that you've done this…but I…well…I fucking love you. So…

GUS. I'm glad. I am so glad you do.

TANNER. I better get going.

GUS. Right. The pupils await.

TANNER. I just…

GUS. What?

TANNER. I hope it doesn't cost you too much.

Tanner walks closer to the painting.

This may be my favorite piece of yours I've seen.

GUS. Yeah?

TANNER. Mmmhmm. It's so true to you. I can feel your voice in it.

GUS. You can?

TANNER. Your work is so ordered and still. This is chaotic. It's furious. It feels like the man I know.

GUS. Oh.

TANNER. I wish the world could know you painted it.

GUS. Yeah. The world is going to love Balkonaé.

TANNER. What about you, Gus.

GUS. I got my wish. I'm in the Parnell.

TANNER. Careful what you ask for.

GUS. For you shall surely get it.

TANNER. …I'm going to be late.

GUS. Will you go with me?

TANNER. …Stupid question.

10.

Jane stands in front of the painting holding a glass of champagne. She is in mid-speech.

JANE. ...I want to welcome you all to the New America show and I ask you to enjoy the art, enjoy the food. The Hat-Trickster's Trio will be performing in the grand hall so go cut a rug in there and please tell your friends about this exhibit. Running until June 29th. Enjoy.

Lights out on Jane. Gus and Tanner enter. They look around at the art.

TANNER. I become acutely aware of just how little money I make when I come to one of these museum openings.

GUS. They're designed to repel the poor. I'm sweating.

TANNER. Is she here?

GUS. I don't see her.

TANNER. Where's the bar? Free wine, Gus.

GUS. My hands are shaking.

TANNER. It's going to be okay.
(Spots Jane.) Uh oh. Jane at twelve o'clock.

GUS. Shit your twelve or mine?

JANE. Gus!

GUS. Jane!

JANE. Welcome! You're looking chic! Kisses!

Cheek kisses.

Muah Muah. Ohhhhh Hello Tanner!

TANNER. Heeeeey Jane.

JANE. So good to see you!

TANNER. We're really...uh...glad we could be here...for you.

JANE. Not bad for my first time out! A lot of press! What do you think of the show so far Gus?

GUS. It's very...diverse.

JANE. RIGHT! So many new voices!

TANNER. It's all very exciting.

JANE. I'm so glad you're here!

GUS. Wouldn't miss it for the world…Uh Jane…I need to talk to you.

JANE. Of course, Gus dear. Oh Wait! Have you seen Balkonaé?

GUS. Not yet. Listen Jane—

JANE. —I know she's here. Tanner have you met Ms. Townsend?

TANNER. Haven't had the pleasure.

GUS. I'm sure she's here. Listen Jane. First I want to apologize for—

JANE. —Oh! Here she is! Here's our Balkonaé!

> *Balkonaé enters. [Note on costume: This ensemble should be a collision of African fabric, hipster chic, and haute couture. Are those things that separate? Anywho, it should be tasteful but certainly fashion forward. It should be impressive but need not be a gown.]*

BALKONAÉ. What's good, what's good!

GUS. Our Balkonaé, huh?

TANNER. Oh. My. GOD.

BALKONAÉ. Can you stand it?

JANE. Tanner Ms. Townsend is fascinating. Gus you really hit gold! *(Notices a wealthy donor.)* I'm sorry I'll be right back! Donor on the run.

> *Jane exits. Balkonaé and Gus stare at each other. Tanner takes in Balkonaé.*

GUS. Balkonaé Tanner Tanner Balkonaé.

BALKONAÉ. Hey there Top Ramen! Gus he's cute! Way too cute for you.

TANNER. I…I'm speechless. Vanessa—

BALKONAÉ. —AhAhAh. No No Miss Thang. We're here to have a good time! Don't you wanna have a good time Tanner?

TANNER. Yes.

BALKONAÉ. There you go! Gus you should be more like your man! Am I right Tan Tan?

TANNER. She's like the best drag queen I've ever seen.

BALKONAÉ. Am I giving you life?! Am I renewing your faith in humanity?

TANNER. I'm so turned on right now.

GUS. Jesus, Tanner!

TANNER. She's like walking sex.

BALKONAÉ. Gus's Boyfriend, have you looked at my paintings.

TANNER. Uh…

BALKONAÉ. Let me walk you through all this genius. Now this… one…this one is called *the cotton is high.*

GUS. What?

BALKONAÉ. And this one right here is called *fly girl, in the milk.* You dig?

GUS. Okay that's enough.

BALKONAÉ. Like my outfit?

GUS. No.

BALKONAÉ. Ooooo somebody has on their sassy pants tonight.

GUS. Congrats.

BALKONAÉ. It's what I do.

GUS. What *you* do? Huh?

TANNER. Maybe we should all just enjoy the show huh?

GUS. No. I want to hear what she has to say.

BALKONAÉ. I paint big ole paintings that explore the expanse of my woman-ness as it intersects and inter-relates with my Blafrican American identity / and sell them.

GUS. / Stop it! You're making a / mockery—

BALKONAÉ. / Stop what Gus?

GUS. You're a fraud.

TANNER. Okay you need to cool it.

BALKONAÉ. That's it? That's all you got?

GUS. I made you! *(Mocking Balkonaé.)* "Yes bitch, Get into me!"

BALKONAÉ. *(Shocked and impressed by Gus' volley back.)* Ooop! Is that how I sound?

GUS. You wouldn't be here without me.

BALKONAÉ. Is that what you think? Just gonna take credit for everything! Even me!

GUS. Yes.

BALKONAÉ. Boy, take a look around here. This is a whole room full of people here to see me!

GUS. Woooooow That's actually what you think?

TANNER. Maybe we should go.

GUS. I'm actually an artist. You're just…pretending.

BALKONAÉ. Dude.

GUS. I AM NOT A DUDE!!!

BALKONAÉ. It don't matter what you think is "true." All that matters is that line out the door. All that matters is that I'm giving the people something they want to see.

GUS. Which is?

TANNER. You both need to end this right now.

BALKONAÉ. No one was checking for you Gus.

GUS. This is all mine. Those paintings I painted.

BALKONAÉ. Well I know that…and you know that…but uh… they don't know that sweetheart. They see my name on those paintings. So what's the truth? Huh? What are they gonna believe, the things right in front of their eyes or some fairytale you cooked up?

GUS. We cooked up!

BALKONAÉ. I mean I understand you being a little jealous maybe—

TANNER. Wait a minute.

BALKONAÉ. But this slander has to stop. It's very unattractive Gus. Don't hate because I'm the better artist.

GUS. HA!

TANNER. This is surreal.

BALKONAÉ. In fact. I'm hurt by this Gus.

GUS. Oh please!

BALKONAÉ. We've worked in the same studio for months now.

GUS. You're not a better artist.

BALKONAÉ. Oh. I'm superior.

TANNER. Don't listen to her.

BALKONAÉ. Just accept it!

GUS. No.

BALKONAÉ. —Say it with me.

GUS. No. You're not even—

BALKONAÉ. —Come on. Say it with me. "Balkonaé wore it better."

GUS. No.

BALKONAÉ. Balkonaé—

GUS. No!

BALKONAÉ. The truth will set you free!

Jane enters.

JANE. Howard Marshall has been running from me for weeks. Had to track him down. Sorry about that. Everything alright.

BALKONAÉ. Everything's great. Just chatting here with Gussy.

GUS. It's just Gus.

BALKONAÉ. I'm gonna try real hard to remember that.

GUS. Considering it's because of me that you're here.

BALKONAÉ. Girl bye.

JANE. Are you two arguing? Cut that out.

GUS. I got something to say.

BALKONAÉ. Do you?

GUS. Yes.

JANE. Well alright.

GUS. I wanted to tell you this in private but…

JANE. Yes?

BALKONAÉ. Tell her.

JANE. Tell me what?

BALKONAÉ. We're all waiting to hear. Tell her.

JANE. What are you two talking about?

BALKONAÉ. About how Gus wanna be me!

GUS. Alright! That's it! This isn't an artist. This is an actress. I hired her! I fooled you! I got you! She's getting paid and you got your black or blafrican or what the hell you are calling her. Open your eyes woman! There! That's the truth. The art you think she made I MADE! I'm the black artist. HA! HA! Put that in ya pipe and smoke it! Boom! You have been HAD!

JANE. Ah.

GUS. HA!

JANE. That's quite the revelation.

GUS. Now kiss my big black ass!

Silence.

BALKONAÉ. You feel better?

JANE. Are you finished?

GUS. Yes.

JANE. Good.

GUS. In your face!

JANE. I knew!

GUS. You…What?

JANE. You think I couldn't figure out what you were up to? I know. I knew. I have always known.

GUS. But—

JANE. —At first I was a little annoyed that you were trying to trick me. I mean…we're friends right? I thought you understood where I was coming from. I thought you supported my passions. It hurt a little. But then…I realized something, Gus. You had given me an incredible opportunity here. What if I could put actual, physical diversity in the museum instead of just its representation? Oh Gus… You're an amazing artist and Balkonaé is your greatest work yet!

GUS. Wait…I…

JANE. You are a genius.

TANNER. I don't understand.

JANE. Balkonaé Townsend is your greatest work of art. She is the art. These paintings? They are just the byproduct of the true artistic triumph. Balkonaé is the real thing. She's something.

TANNER. Oh my god.

GUS. Wait…Jane…I didn't make her.

JANE. Sure you did.

BALKONAÉ. *(Vanessa?)* No he didn't.

JANE. You made her. You named her. Isn't this what you wanted me to do Gus? Isn't this why you went to such great lengths?

GUS. No!

BALKONAÉ. Listen lady…You must have bumped you head if you think—

JANE. —The crowds are going to love you.

BALKONAÉ. Huh?

JANE. It's okay…This is a good thing! Let's celebrate! Cheers!

GUS. I…

JANE. Yes?

GUS. If you knew why did you let this happen?

JANE. I'm interested in the cutting edge. I don't want something simple. I want work that's complicated. That's hard. That's not easy to understand. You have made art out of personality. Actual persona. You formed her.

VANESSA. I'm not art.

JANE. Of course! You are you. *(To Gus.)* We are adding her to our permanent collection.

VANESSA. No…I'm a person. A whole person.

JANE. Ahhhhh. So REAL!

VANESSA. Like a human being.

JANE. Yes, you are! Yes. This is the most exciting piece we have acquired in years.

VANESSA. I'm not staying in here!

JANE. It's really quite cozy. I think you'll like it.

GUS. How much?

TANNER. Gus have you lost your mind?

GUS. I want to know. I want to know how much.

JANE. A lot. You're going to make a lot of money and will be fêted years to come.

TANNER. You can't just keep her here.

JANE. Sure we can.

BALKONAÉ. How much am I worth.

TANNER. YOUPEOPLEARECRAZY!!!!!! I can't take it anymore! We're leaving!

> *Tanner begins to exit; he pulls Gus with him. Balkonaé stops him.*

BALKONAÉ. Wait. *(To Jane.)* What are you going to do with me?

JANE. Set you up really nice in the east wing. Full environment. Your natural habitat.

BALKONAÉ. All the people will walk by and watch me?

JANE. They'll press their faces against the glass to get a closer look.

BALKONAÉ. For as long as I live.

JANE. Yes!

GUS. She's gonna put you on display!

TANNER. Let's go Gus.

JANE. For all to see.

GUS. Vanessa.

BALKONAÉ. Shhhh…

GUS. You can't breath under glass!

JANE. The crowd is waiting for you. Are you ready Balkonaé?

BALKONAÉ. I wanted to—

JANE. —Gus, are you coming with us?

TANNER. Hell no! Come on Gus.

GUS. No.

TANNER. What?

JANE. It's time Balkonaé.

BALKONAÉ. Right.

> *A beat. Gus takes Tanner's hand; they watch.*

JANE. *(To the crowd.)* Ladies and gentlemen. The woman you have been waiting to hear from… Balkonaé Townsend.

> *Balkonaé walks in front of Gus' all-white chaotic painting.*
> *Applause.*
> *Balkonaé stands before the painting.*
> *She looks at it.*
> *Then she looks at the audience. She is nervous. She steadies herself.*
> *Then:*

BALKONAÉ. I want to thank you all for…

> *Vanessa tries to speak from inside. Balkonaé holds her back.*

It is so great to see you all here to share in the work that…

> *Vanessa tries again. This internal conflict should worsen over the proceeding.*

That…

> *Vanessa's face pushes its way to the surface, holds, then recedes.*

That I have…

> *Vanessa is fighting very hard to get out!*

For so long I have worked to bring this—

> *Finally. Vanessa emerges. This battle between Vanessa and Balkonaé is all internal. Vanessa perhaps gains control of parts of Balkonaé's body. The struggle should feel like a strangling, a wringing, an exorcism, a moment of ecstasy. All of the violence is inside but it should shake the actress physically in a very real way!*

VANESSA. —Could we compromise on who gets to drive—

BALKONAÉ. —Excuse me…I'm sorry…Where was I…the work—

VANESSA. —There are some things I have to say that are—

BALKONAÉ. —I started out thinking about the complexity of identity and how I could—

VANESSA. —Don't forget about me. I have helped you Balkonaé—

BALKONAÉ. —You? Help me?—

VANESSA. —Yes. Let's just work together girl. Don't shut me—

BALKONAÉ. —The work grows out of my experience growing up in a predominately—

VANESSA. —I'm Here! Don't you feel me—

BALKONAÉ. —When I began my work in Gus McKnight's studio—

VANESSA. —Let me out! Let me out!—

BALKONAÉ. —I'm here now—

VANESSA. —SO AM I—

BALKONAÉ. I don't want to die.

VANESSA. You won't.

BALKONAÉ. I won't?

VANESSA. We are both here.

BALKONAÉ. Yeah?

VANESSA. Yeah girl. You my backbone.

BALKONAÉ. I came from you.

VANESSA. You hold me up. You make me talk back. You know my rights.

BALKONAÉ. Make a little more room for me, okay?

VANESSA. And you for me.

BALKONAÉ. We are both making each other.

VANESSA. We been making each other.

BALKONAÉ. What you wanna do?

VANESSA. Make it plain for 'em.

BALKONAÉ. You think they can handle it girl.

VANESSA. We been carrying it.

BALKONAÉ. *(AND VANESSA???)* Alright. Alright. As…As I… was saying. This work comes from my experience: trying to fit in. The times when I felt alone. In a sea of white. Miles and miles of white that I was expected to be a part of. To live inside of. That…is the impetus for all of my art.

When you press your fingers and faces against the cold glass to see me. When you snap pictures of me and place them online. When you take my fat ass and thick lips and staple them to your bodies. When you look at me and watch me…do you see me? Smiling at first. Gentle even. Loving perhaps. Be careful. I could want to open up to you and allow the raging sea inside me to pour out all over this planet. Then what the hell we gone do?

> *She puts her index and middle finger in her mouth like a handgun. She cocks. She pulls the "trigger." A red paint splatter hits the white painting. She look at us. She turns and looks at the painting. She has made the best art we have seen. She looks back to us. She smiles...no...smirks. Perhaps she laughs. Hold... Get into how dope she is. Then everything slams to black.*

That's It.

PROPERTY LIST
(Use this space to create props lists for your production)

SOUND EFFECTS

(Use this space to create sound effects lists for your production)

Note on Songs/Recordings, Images, or Other Production Design Elements

Be advised that Dramatists Play Service, Inc., neither holds the rights to nor grants permission to use any songs, recordings, images, or other design elements mentioned in the play. It is the responsibility of the producing theater/organization to obtain permission of the copyright owner(s) for any such use. Additional royalty fees may apply for the right to use copyrighted materials.

For any songs/recordings, images, or other design elements mentioned in the play, works in the public domain may be substituted. It is the producing theater/organization's responsibility to ensure the substituted work is indeed in the public domain. Dramatists Play Service, Inc., cannot advise as to whether or not a song/arrangement/recording, image, or other design element is in the public domain.